The Busy Woman's Little Book of Motivation

42 Morsels of Motivation To Help You Live Out Loud and Become The Phenomenal Woman You Were Born To Be

Cassandra Mack

Authors Choice Press
New York Lincoln Shanghai

The Busy Woman's Little Book of Motivation
42 Morsels of Motivation To Help You Live Out Loud and Become
The Phenomenal Woman You Were Born To Be

Copyright © 2007, 2008 by Cassandra Mack

Authors Choice Press
an imprint of iUniverse, Inc.

iUniverse books may be ordered through booksellers or by contacting:

iUniverse
2021 Pine Lake Road, Suite 100
Lincoln, NE 68512
www.iuniverse.com
1-800-Authors (1-800-288-4677)

Because of the dynamic nature of the Internet, any Web addresses or links contained in this book may have changed since publication and may no longer be valid.

The views expressed in this work are solely those of the author and do not necessarily reflect the views of the publisher, and the publisher hereby disclaims any responsibility for them.

Originally published by My company, Strategies for Empowered Liv

ISBN: 978-0-595-49780-5

Printed in the United States of America

Contents

Chapter 6. Taking Steps Towards Healthier Relationships

Introduction

They say that writing is cathartic. This I have found to be true. Because while it may seem like I am writing solely for others, I now know that I am also writing for me. What I want more than anything is to live as fully as I can while balancing the many competing priorities that I face as a woman – a woman living in a world that moves at an insanely fast pace and that pressures me to look outside myself for the things that bring me fulfillment and joy.

I knew that I was not the only woman in the world who needed to stop living life by default. I also knew I wasn't the only woman who felt frazzled and overwhelmed and who needed an occasional pick-me-up or reality check. I knew I was not alone in this experience.

As women, we wear many hats. Some of us are wives and mothers. We're daughters, sisters, girlfriends, and continual works-in-progress. Speaking for myself, I play so many parts and carry out so many different roles that I have to work diligently to not allow myself to fall into the Super Woman trap – because none of us can be all things to all people.

In my professional life, I'm a keynote speaker and workshop leader conducting seminars and classes that help others put plans in place to achieve their personal and professional goals. I'm an advocate helping women and girls own their power and speak their truths. I'm a writer, putting my thoughts on paper for others to read, mull over and hopefully become inspired by. But at the end of the day I'm just a woman trying to do the best I can to walk my talk.

The reason I teach and speak about personal empowerment is not because I am a master. It's because I am on the journey with you – striving to become more, grow more and live more authentically.

The Busy Woman's Little Book of Motivation is a collection of insightful lessons and anecdotes that will help you own your power, keep the cup full enough to feed yourself, get in the driver's seat of your career, let go of the ledge, break the habit of self-sabotage and take steps toward healthier relationships.

Writing *The Busy Woman's Little Book of Motivation* has brought me to the awareness that your attitude and outlook along with the ability to be totally honest about your stress, mess and drama play a significant role in getting the results you want. Let today be the day that you position yourself to live more powerfully, joyfully and authentically. I'll be rooting for you.

See you on the path,
Cassandra Mack

Special Note From The Author

You are reading the revised edition of *The Busy Woman's Little Book of Motivation.*

In our excitement and enthusiasm to get the book out to women everywhere as quickly as possible, we sent the draft copy of *The Busy Woman's Little Book of Motivation* to print, which was not sufficiently ready for the general public. In lieu of this oversight, we donated the 1st printing of *The Busy Woman's Little Book of Motivation* to nonprofit organizations that serve women in need.

In this revised edition, we've including a book discussion guide and tips for starting your own women's reading circle. If you have started your own women's reading circle and you are using this book to generate dialogue, please visit me on the web at: **www.strategiesforempoweredliving.com** and share your experiences by posting on my blog or calling into my radio show The No More Drama Hour Of Power, which is aired live every Monday from 12noon to 1pm, eastern standard time and can be accessed from my website as well.

Chapter 1.
Owning Your Power

Motivational Morsel #1.
Decide What You Want and Have The Audacity To Go After It

What's the one thing you want in life more than anything else? What is the one thing that would make you happier, more fulfilled, more contented and fuel your sense of passion? No matter what you want to do, be or have in life the process of attaining it starts with figuring out what you want. Then transforming this wish into a burning desire that propels you to take continual and consistent action.

People who are often no more talented or skilled than others, but who have the audacity to go after the things they want in life, usually end up getting them. Why? They make up their minds to become unstoppable, to rise above adversity, to let nothing stand in their way. They dedicate their time and resources to the attainment of their goals. They plan to succeed and when obstacles come their way, they figure out a way to overcome them or work around them.

Deciding what you want is the single most important step in living the life you desire, but most of us get stuck at this critical stage because we can't see how the life we want is possible, so we allow limited vision and lack of clarity to cause us to give up before we ever get started. Don't sabotage yourself this way. Don't worry if you don't have all the pieces pulled together just yet, or if you can't figure out how the life you want is possible.

What is most important is that you have an idea of what you want. Then you can transform your idea into an intense burning desire, that will develop into a vision, which in time will be narrowed down into a purpose-driven goal.

See the way the mind works is you must first decide what you want, then your mind will figure out a way to help you get it. Once you firmly decide what you want, you will begin to attract the people, resources and ideas that will enable you to achieve the things you long to achieve.

Today, spend some time thinking about what you really want. Write it down. Then have the audacity to go after it.

Motivational Morsel #2.
Honor The Life You Have Now

Few women know how great they truly are. We focus too much on what's wrong with us rather than acknowledge what's right about us. Truth be told, many of us daydream about living a perfect life or trading ourselves in for a new and improved version. The problem with this way of thinking is it sets us up to slumber through life treating it like a dress rehearsal, putting our plans and dreams on hold until everything becomes perfect. We must realize that things will never be perfect, because real life is not perfect. Life is a constant flow of peaks and valleys, where you celebrate the peaks, ride out the valleys, and hopefully learn some important lessons along the way.

Acknowledging what's good about you is not about being haughty or vain. It's about honoring the woman you are today, respecting the life you have now and approaching your life with a sense of gratitude, even if you don't have everything you want.

Speaking for myself, it took me a long time to grasp the importance of honoring the life I have now. I was so busy being a workaholic, goalaholic and perfectionist that I failed to appreciate the journey. As a result, I was often left frustrated, and frazzled. And, I felt like who I was, was never enough. I was so busy planning the perfect life that I did not allow myself to fully live. Don't fall into this trap. Be patient with yourself as you evolve into the woman you were born to be. Above all else, while planning for the future, appreciate the present. Because you only get one shot at life. And when it's over, it's over.

Today, make yourself a promise that you will live each day as fully as you can and no matter where you are on the journey you will dare to live with passion. Celebrate the woman you are today.

Motivational Morsel #3.
Don't Apologize For Your Success

It's hard to accept that there are some people who will be uncomfortable with your success – so much so that they will start to avoid you, dismiss your ideas, subtly try to tear you down and speak death to your dreams before they have a chance to blossom. They notice that you're changing, thinking bigger, taking more risks, laying claim to your vision, stepping out on faith and they resent you for it... often without even knowing why.

For many of us, this realization is so painful that we go to great lengths to dim our light and downplay our dreams. But in doing so we hold ourselves back.

Fear of success, not failure, has derailed more dreams than anything else. Why? Because it requires that we take the road less traveled. And when you take the road less traveled, you will no longer fit the life you've come to know. You'll be the odd one out. You'll outgrow some of the people who started on the journey with you. And this can be quite uncomfortable, because nobody wants to walk their path alone.

The good news is success breeds success. So it's only a matter of time before you connect with people who will encourage you, inspire you and motivate you to soar higher. Don't worry about the haters, nay-sayers and perpetrators. They come with the territory.

Focus on your plans and dreams. Allow yourself to think big, long for more and go after your goals with everything you've got. And when you finally achieve your plans and dreams make no apologies for it.

Motivational Morsel #4.
Go At Your Own Pace

I can remember being so afraid of not "making it" by a certain point in time that I obsessively worked myself to a state of exhaustion trying to reach this impossible deadline so that I could prove to others how much I had it going on and how much I had arrived. As long as fear of not "making it" by a specified time was my motive, I could never do enough, work enough, plan enough, or earn enough, to satisfy the voice of doubt and insecurity that lived inside my head. I thought about what "they had" and what "they achieved." Then I thought about what I did not have and did not achieve. And whenever I compared where I was against where I thought they were, I never seemed to measure up.

What I failed to realize back then was success comes in many forms. And whenever we measure our lives against the lives of those around us we will always come up short. Why? Because the only true measure of your success is the one you make against your own potential. Are you celebrating who you are and what you have achieved in your own right or are you wondering and worrying about what other people have?

Trying to keep up with the Jones's is like drinking from a never-ending cup of envy and insecurity. You'll always thirst for more and nothing you do will ever be enough.

Before you drive yourself crazy obsessing over what other people have, always remember that appearances can be deceiving and everything that glitters ain't gold. The woman at the office who always looks flawlessly pulled together may be two paychecks away from an eviction notice. The couple who has the corner house, luxury car, and the kid at Harvard may be in a loveless marriage where they tolerate each other, but behind closed doors can't stand the sight of one another. The beautiful woman who all the other women secretly hate may be so lonely and broken, that she'll do anything to the point of degradation just to be held for the night.

14

It's foolish to say that we will never have moments of envy or that we'll never look at someone else's life and ask, *"why not me?"* But if you could try to be a little more patient with yourself and focus on all the good things that you have to offer as well as the many ways that you are blessed, sooner than you know it, your life will come together in a way that feels right for you and you will make greater strides. Today, be thankful for what you've got and go at your own pace. In due time you will get where you need to go.

Motivational Morsel #5
Come As You Are

People have a funny way of discounting those who have fallen on hard times, who struggle with an issue or two or who have made a mistake that is so publicly humiliating that they can barely enter a room without a condescending whisper or a back-handed stare.

Before we judge ourselves too harshly, it's important to keep in mind that everyone has a blind spot, a point of weakness, an area of personal struggle that causes us to trip and fall. Nobody's perfect. Everyone is trying to find their own way the best way that they know how. So don't walk around with your head hanging down because you've got a few issues, you're not where you want to be or you are so knee deep in the middle of your mess that it would take a tractor and two shovels to dig you out.

Life does not require us to be perfect. But it does require us to show up and come as we are. Your growth is your business. Just because you've got some growing to do does not mean that you cannot take steps towards your success or allow yourself to serve as a blessing to others.

And in case you are still in doubt about your ability to be of service while you are in the midst of your own struggles, here are a few biblical examples of people who were flawed but who served and inspired none-the-less. Moses had a speech impediment and struggled with insecurity, but God used him to lead a nation out of bondage. Noah had an appetite for alcohol, but God used him to build the Ark and repopulate the earth. Rahab was a prostitute, but she was instrumental in helping the Israelites win victory over Jericho. King Solomon had a weakness for women, yet he wrote the book of proverbs.

What did all of these individuals have in common? They came as they were... with all of their stress, mess and drama. And in spite of themselves, they achieved great things.

It's easy to believe that you cannot move in the direction of your mission until every "i" is dotted every "t" is crossed and all your ducks are lined up in a row. But if you come as you are and let God work out the rest you can be used mightily and achieve monumental results.

While people may be quick to judge you, talk about you, think they're better than you and place limits on who you are and what you can achieve, God is not a respecter of persons and will use whatever and whoever is necessary to fulfill the larger purpose.

So today, pick yourself up, dust yourself up and don't obsess over your weaknesses and issues. Just be willing to be of service. And if anyone has the nerve to stand in judgment of you...hold your head up high, focus on what you've been called to do and let he who is perfect and blameless, get up and cast the first stone.

Motivational Morsel #6.
Be Your Own Cheerleader

It's great to have people in your life who believe in you and cheer you on. People who are genuinely interested in what you are trying to achieve and who support you in all of your goals and endeavors.

Each of us need people in our lives who give us that much needed vote of encouragement so that we can feel confident in our capabilities and move forward toward our goals. But every now and then, there will be times in your life when there is no one around to stand up and cheer you on.

When this happens, you must resist the inclination to throw a pity party. Instead, become your own cheerleader. Encourage yourself. Boost your own morale. Coach yourself as if you were speaking to a star athlete. Give yourself a motivational pep talk. Champion your own cause. Why? Because, nobody knows your strengths and talents better than you and no one can motivate you better than you. So from this day forward, develop an attitude of positive expectancy and prophesy over your own life. Today, declare our loud...I am stepping into my greatness and many good things await me!!!

Motivational Morsel # 7.
Get Out Of Your Own Way

Many times when we set out to do, be or have something, we compile a mental list of reasons why our ideas won't fly, our plans won't work and why our dreams will not come into fruition. We think about past failures and previous attempts, then make a case of why it's not the right time to go after the things we want out of life. When we engage in this type of behavior we are the block that blocks, our blessings. In essence, we are standing in our own way.

Every dream that you have, every goal that you set is a preview of what's possible for you. If it were not possible, your mind would not conceive it. Those who replace doubt with determination and fear with faith eventually come to realize their ambitions despite past failures, criticism or adverse circumstances.

It's easy to get stuck in your comfort zone and resist the things in life that are challenging or unfamiliar. But always remember that there is a fine line between being cautious and living in fear. When you allow your rational and responsible self to drown out the voice of your curious and courageous self, you start to live a life that feels stale and stifling.

If you want to reclaim your life, and live more authentically, let your curious and courageous self be your guide. Right now list three things that you would love to do but seem beyond your comfort zone. What new experiences would you like to have? What new things would you like to try?

When you take steps towards the things you want in life what you are really saying is, *I am serious about living my best life.* And in doing so, you empower yourself in a tangible way. Today, remind yourself that you hold the key that unlocks the door to your most powerful, phenomenal life.

Chapter 2.
Keeping The Cup Full
Enough To Feed Yourself

Motivational Morsel #8.
Even Superwoman Had To Take Off The Cape

As women, we are blessed with a remarkable gift called resourcefulness, and we've got the multi-tasking skill down to an art form. We raise our children, support our partners, encourage our friends and families, give our all on the job and still find time to contribute to our places of worship as well as the larger community. As wonderful as it is to nurture and give, far too many of us give at the expense of our own self-care.

Many of us are at the point where we are overwhelmed and overextended, because we take on too much and try to be all things to all people. We're giving way too much of ourselves without reserving anything for self. We've been led to believe that busyness equals productivity. And the more we take on the more fulfilling our lives become. But the truth is living a nonstop, overextended life only leads you to a place of crash and burn.

We are socialized to believe that a bigger house, more money, a new car, or a fabulous wardrobe can fulfill that sense of contentment that we're longing for on the inside. But more and more we are finding, that working at an insane pace and trying to win the rat race just doesn't cut it anymore. If you want to live life at a saner pace, you have to make it a priority to tend to your mental, physical, emotional and spiritual needs, otherwise your life will continue to feel chaotic and unfulfilling. A big part of what keeps us happy and healthy is taking good care of ourselves.

Rituals of self-nurturance are the glue that holds sane, savvy women together. With this idea in mind, consider two simple self-nurturing rituals that you can incorporate into your daily or weekly regimen in order to pamper yourself and keep yourself from going into overdrive.

Start treating yourself better by thinking about simple things that you can do at work and at home to avoid the Superwoman trap. Re-train your family and friends to respect your, "me time." Learn to say no. If saying no is difficult for you, ask yourself this question: *What is it costing me to keep saying yes?*

Motivational Morsel #9.
Make Time For Quiet Contemplation

I resisted making time for quiet contemplation for a long time. My excuses were: (1.) I have too much on my plate already and cannot afford to put one more item on my to-do-list. (2.) I am sleep deprived as it is and do not want to wake up any earlier than necessary. (3.) Quiet contemplation is a waste of time that could be better spent engaging in an activity that brings me immediate value.

But I kept discovering that when I allowed myself to get quiet and go deep within, I would come out with renewed insight, a new revelation, greater clarity, and a spirit of peace and assuredness that would set the tone for the rest of my day. Sometimes these insights and feelings came immediately. Other times they came hours, days or weeks after. But the common denominator was the process of quiet contemplation offered me tremendous benefits.

Life is always in motion. And there will always be one thing or another that needs your attention, but if you take the time to tune out the noise of the world so that you can better hear your quiet promptings and longings, your life will begin to feel more authentic.

If an hour feels like too much, try a half hour. Starting tomorrow, try to spend one hour going within. You can write your thoughts in a journal, pray, sit in silence with a cup of coffee or tea, read your favorite text, plan your day, listen attentively or wait in expectation, or anything else that enables you to quietly contemplate. The key here is to get more in touch with you.

Motivational Morsel #10.
Define Your Priorities

A priority is anything that is important to you. Priorities are not necessarily written in stone, but they do provide you with a point of focus. When setting your priorities, allow some room for flexibility because depending on where you are and what you are dealing with, your needs and goals will change. I find it helpful to think of priorities as personal commitments that give purpose to each day and move you in the direction of your goals. And believe it or not, the more that you've got on your plate, the more important it becomes to define your priorities and not allow yourself to get sidetracked.

Many of us assume that we can lead productive lives by just going with the flow. Well we can't. While it's perfectly ok to go with the flow every now and then, it's also important that we have plans and set tasks. Because if we do not define our priorities, we can easily get caught up in somebody else's agenda.

Many women, myself included, have difficulty defining and sticking to their priorities. With so many competing priorities pulling you in different directions, it seems like everything needs your immediate attention. But the reality is that there is only one of you to go around and your time is in limited supply. And in order to manage the many items on your to-do-list and keep the cup from running over, you need to be diligently disciplined around who and what you give your time, and attention to.

This week, make a list of your priorities for the week. Then break them down daily, and make the commitment to stick to them. We can always find reasons to not define and stick to our priorities and to allow ourselves to get sidetracked, but when we stick to the priorities that matter to us, not only are we respecting our time, we are respecting our lives as well.

Motivational Morsel #11.
Identify What's Draining You

In a Personal Power seminar that I led for a group of female managers in Chicago, I asked women to identify the things in their lives that were draining them. I had them make out a list and rate the severity of the energy drain on a scale of 1 to 10 with 1 being slightly stressful and 10 being draining to the point of toxicity.

I was surprised to discover that most of the things that drained the women in this seminar were things that were within their control like: a friend, or family member who made unreasonable demands on their time, a job were they felt undervalued and unappreciated, being on a committee that took up too much of their time with no direct benefit, putting off making decisions that needed to be made, holding on to feelings of rage and bitterness, living in clutter, a loveless relationship where they simply tolerated their partner or having to go through a major life issue without adequate support.

When you identify and let go of the things that drain you, you free up the mental and emotional energy needed to attract more positive experiences into your life. Not only will you feel better, you will become more productive and effective in all other areas of your life.

As women, we've got to be vigilant about noticing the things in our lives that weigh heavily on us and stunt our growth. Then, we have to make the necessary changes to plug the energy drains in our lives like: setting boundaries with others, standing up for ourselves when people try to take advantage of us or cross the line, making sure we put a support system in place, making the tough decisions that need to be made, getting organized and stepping away from people and situations that keep us stuck or bring us down.

If we do not identify the energy drains, they'll only get bigger and bigger until we are so burnt out that we are no good to ourselves. This week, focus on eliminating some of the energy drains in your life and watch how your life begins to open up to more positive, powerful experiences.

Motivational Morsel #12.
The World Can't Give You Happiness and The World Can't Take It Away

How happy are you right now? Do you even know? Perhaps you think you'll be happier when you get a bigger house, a better paying job, lose that extra thirty pounds or find someone wonderful to share your life with. Most women, myself included, treat happiness as the prize we win for achieving our goals or a euphoric feeling that comes from something outside of ourselves. But true happiness is a state of mind that we can consciously choose by becoming more aware of the little things in life that put a smile on our face and make us feel contented on the inside.

The reason so many of us believe that happiness comes from external things and accolades is we've become over stimulated by a world that glorifies excess and the external. It's easy to lose sight of what really matters, when we are constantly bombarded with images that tell us we need something outside of ourselves to be happy and whole. But if we are to live happy and fulfilled lives, we've got to commit to making our happiness a personal priority.

Today, ask yourself: What do I need to be truly happy? Spend some time thinking about this question. Be reflective and contemplative as you uncover the answer. Trust that the answer to this question lies inside of you and that authentic happiness is within your grasp.

And when you find the answer, bask in the realization that...*The world can't give it to you, so the world can't take it away.*

<u>Motivational Morsel #13.</u>
Get Your House In Order

Because we dread it, many of us put off getting our house in order until the piles of dust and clutter are so high that we literally feel overwhelmed and out of sorts by the piling mess and chaos. When we have orderly and reasonably neat homes, we are able to think clearer, restore a sense of order to our daily endeavors and we don't have to shriek in embarrassment if someone happens to unexpectedly drop by.

Order impacts just about every aspect of daily living especially your day-to-day activities. It's difficult to enjoy a nice meal at your dining room table, account for your bills, go over homework or simply get clear and centered if you have piles of paper and junk laying around. Believe it or not, how we care for our homes is a subtle expression of how we care for ourselves.

We need to run our homes instead of allowing clutter and disorder to run us. If you are guilty of living in clutter here is a simple rule to live by: Figure out what reasonably neat and orderly means to you. Better yet, pretend your mother-in-law was coming to visit and let that standard serve as your guide. Creating an orderly home really does bring order and clarity to the other areas of your life.

Motivational Morsel #14.
Recognize That Your Days Are Numbered

We've all heard the saying: *live each day as if it were your last.* But most of us treat our lives as if we had an infinite amount of time. We move through life as if we will receive advance notice of when our time is up. We put off so much, delay so many dreams and waste too many precious hours on people and things that don't deserve our time and attention.

When you treat each day as if it were your last, the past no longer holds you captive and you don't stress and obsess over what tomorrow might bring. And most importantly, you don't take the ordinary, seemingly unimportant things for granted. You simply cherish each day as a gift.

It's only when we truly understand that our days are numbered, that we start to live more richly, fully and appreciatively. We start to embrace and savor the simple mundane experiences like: sipping a fresh brewed cup of coffee, seeing a garden in full bloom, spending time with loved ones, chatting on the phone with an old friend, a warm relaxing bath, walking in the rain, seeing a first snow fall.

Whenever I get stuck in a funk that I just can't seem to pull myself out of, I visit an old cemetery. The stillness of it all reminds me that when it's over, it's over. So my best bet is to pick myself up, pull myself out of my little funk and recognize that everyday above ground is certainly better than any day below it.

So until it is carved out in stone, you've been blessed with a tremendous gift called life. Honor this gift by living each day as fully as you can.

Chapter 3.
Getting In The Driver's Seat
of Your Career

Motivational Morsel #15
Map Out A Plan For Learning, Growing and Advancing

If someone were to ask you: Where do you see yourself in five years, what would you say? Would you be able to articulate a clear deliberate plan, for learning, growing and advancing in your career?

The key to getting ahead and staying on top of your game is having a plan. Having a plan enables you to move your career in the direction that you want it to go in. It's about taking the initiative to bring your goals and plans into fruition. And this puts you in the driver's seat of your career.

Here are 8 tips that will help you map out a plan.

1. Identify the most important attributes that you will need to advance to the next two levels. Figure out where you measure up. Then, develop a game plan to close the gap between where you are now and where you want to be two years from now.
2. Identify your goals. What do you want to do, be and have in life and what do you need to do to get there? Write down the steps you'll need to take.
3. Identify two to three new skills you would like to learn and map out a plan to learn them.
4. Turn your car or subway ride into a mini-learning center by listening to professional development and personal enrichment audio programs.
5. Seek out a mentor. Find someone who is further along in her career and schedule regular meetings by phone, e-mail or in-person to discus your goals and plans.
6. Start a mastermind group. Meet with 5 to 7 success-minded people at least once a month. Share ideas and

give each other feedback on how to advance professionally.

7. Have a purpose in all that you do. Be purposeful about your relationships, how you spend your time as well as the projects and assignments that you take on.

8. Don't wait to be noticed. Keep upper management abreast of the ways you add value, successful projects that you've completed and anything thing else that could help in the advancement of your career.

Motivational Morsel #16.
Make Office Politics Work For You

What's the number one business strategy that will help you get ahead in your career quicker than any other? Understanding office politics. Knowing how to play the political game.

Many women shy away from office politics because they confuse being politically savvy with backbiting and underhandedness. But, becoming politically savvy is really about recognizing that in many ways the workplace is like a game. It has rules, norms and values. It has winners and losers. And the majority of people who are on the losing side do not lose out because they aren't skilled or talented; they lose out because they are not adept at navigating the political maze.

Making office politics work for you is not about being cut throat or compromising your core values. It's about having a solid understanding of your organization's culture, a clear picture of the formal and informal expectations and avoiding the kinds of mistakes that can come back to bite you in the butt.

You may not be a politician, but if you want to thrive and rise in your company, then it's a good idea to learn how to navigate your organization's political maze. The added benefit is the more you know about how things "really work" in your company, the better able you will be to get things done and tailor your work style, professional practices and image to fit within the confines of your organization's culture. And if the culture of your organization is not in alignment with your values and beliefs, you'll have enough information to make the kind of career moves that fit with who you are and where you want to be.

Understanding office politics is a win/win situation no matter how you look at it.

1. How would you describe your organization's culture? If you

had to describe it in ten words or less, what would you say?

2. On a scale of 1 – 10, how savvy are you at navigating the political maze at your place of business?

3. What can you do to become more politically savvy? What are the real rules concerning: time and attendance, how the work gets done, how workers bond and interact with one another, who gets promoted and who get derailed? What do the answers to these questions tell you about the culture of your organization?

Motivational Morsel #17.
Cultivate Strategic Alliances

I'm sure you've heard the phrase: *It's not what you know, it's who you know that counts.* And in many instances this is true. Cultivating strategic alliances now and in the future is critical to your success. Why? Because, your personal and professional success is dependent on other people. No one is an island. You can only go so far alone. We all need support, encouragement and feedback from others in order to expand our network and flourish in the pursuit of our goals.

There are many advantages to building strategic alliances. For starters, you'll have a team of people who can aid you in reaching your professional goals. Second, you'll be exposed to important information and resources that can help you accelerate your career. Third, you'll be more of an asset to your company, because a larger network means more social capital to draw from.

With this in mind, here are 7 things that you can do to cultivate strategic alliances.

1. Identify key people at work and in your professional network who can assist you in meeting your career goals and who can help establish your reputation as someone who's a mover and shaker or who is rapidly on the rise.
2. Seek out a mentor and ask her to show you the ropes and give you feedback on what you can do to increase your value and visibility.
3. Develop a partnership with people in your organization who appear to be favored by upper management and learn as much as you can from them.
4. Be polite to everyone, at every level from the receptionist and custodian to the CEO. You never know who's watching you and you never know who can assist you in reaching your goals.

5. Let people know that they can count on you to be competent, dependable and discreet.
6. Watch others who have a large professional and personal network and incorporate some of the skills they use to broaden your own network
7. If you're extremely shy, take a networking workshop or read a book on effective networking.

Motivational Morsel #18.
Project An Image That Communicates Confidence Competence and Credibility

Studies show that 55 percent of your credibility comes from how you look, 38 percent from how you sound and 7 percent is based on what you say. So in essence if you do not look the part of a competent and credible professional, you may not be perceived that way, no matter how educated, experienced or skilled you are. The good news is your image is the easiest thing to change and you can do so by consciously crafting the kind of image that fits with how you want to be perceived and the kind of reputation that you want to build.

Projecting an image that communicates confidence, competence and credibility starts with developing an unshakable belief in yourself and your ability to achieve the things you want to achieve. It's important to develop the mindset that you are where you are today, because you've earned the right to be there. This inner attitude of self-assurance will give you the necessary confidence to project you most powerful image.

The second thing that will help you to craft your best image is to consistently ask for feedback. Most people will not voluntarily give you feedback, because they don't want to risk offending you, it never occurred to them to tell you what they really think or they simply do not care. So to get honest and open feedback, you are going to have to ask for it, and make it safe for the other person to tell you how they honestly feel. Some powerful questions to ask are:

- Is there anything about the way I dress, speak or act that might be holding me back professionally?

- What suggestions would you make in each area in order for me to accelerate my growth?

- What projects or assignments should I be seeking out? What skills do I need to learn? What else do I need to learn?
- What books would you recommend I read?
- What additional training would you recommend I get?

And here's the most important aspect of handling feedback: There's only one appropriate response and it's "thank you." Don't get bent out of shape if people give you critical feedback. Remember, you asked. Look at feedback as a free coaching session and information that you can use to step up your game. With this idea in mind, here are 4 tips that you can use to project your most powerful image.

1. Do an honest self-assessment. Where can it be said that you need to step it up in order to project your best image?
2. Dress for success. Be sure to observe your company's dress code. Don't just dress for the position you currently have, dress for the position you want. Make sure your clothing, make-up, hair and accessories convey the kind of image that you want to convey.
3. Adopt a role model. One of my role models is Oprah Winfrey. Although I've never met her. The message I get from watching her is "use your life responsibly." I take this message to heart and use it as a guide for my actions.
4. Be the consummate professional. Be professional in your attitude, attire, behavior as well as your verbal and written communication.

Motivational Morsel #19.
Raise Your Visibility

Cheryl was an upwardly mobile career woman who was sharp and highly skilled. She was good at her job. So much so, that most of the other managers often came to her for advice and input. Although Cheryl was smart and knowledgeable, she often complained about being passed over for key assignments and not getting the recognition that she deserved. But here is where the problem was, although Cheryl was sharp and savvy, she rarely volunteered for high-profile projects that showcased her skills or put her in front of key decision makers. Instead, she stayed in the background and allowed others to use up her ideas.

In order to get the recognition and credit you deserve, you've got to raise your visibility. Be seen as a major player. Let others see your true worth and pay attention to your ideas. Everything you do, everything you say and everything you write, provides you with an opportunity to raise your visibility.

With this in mind, here are 7 tips to help you raise your visibility:

1. Get connected to highly visible people. Connecting with highly visible people enables you to attract the attention of those who can assist you in your career goals.
2. Try to find out how others perceive you. Get a clear sense of what upper management, your employees and your board think of you. Be sure to present the kind of image that will keep you in the inner circle and get you invited to key events.
3. When you join professional associations, don't just attend a meeting or two. Volunteer to spearhead a committee or a special project. Many professional associations sponsor conferences and conventions where you can present a workshop or moderate a panel discussion. This promotes positive visibility.

4. Design and conduct a training workshop on a subject that you're highly experienced in or extremely passionate about.
5. Volunteer to plan and organize a company fundraiser.
6. Develop a company wide in-house training program for new hires.
7. Build an impeccable reputation that gets your work noticed. Be known as the individual who delivers high-quality work on schedule and on budget. The key here is to let others see you for the virtual indispensable gem that you are.

Motivational Morsel # 20.
Know Your Market Value

One of the primary reasons why we as women do not get paid what we are worth is we don't know our market value. And since we don't know our market value, we give our ideas and services away too freely. Some of us habitually volunteer for low profile projects that have no direct pay off. Some of us don't ask for raises and perks like we should. And if we are in business for ourselves, we usually undercharge for our services, then complain about how our clients don't value the work that we do.

Knowing your market value is critical to building wealth. It will enable you to learn what you need to learn so that you can live comfortably and take care of the things that you need to take care of. The key to knowing your market value involves two things: First, finding out what the median pay is for your job function at your level of skill, expertise and experience. Second, assessing how your skills, strengths and expertise add value to your company and clients. If you are not sure what your market value is go on line and do a Goggle Search for your job function in your state. This will give you a clearer idea of what you should be getting paid.

Additionally, every quarter you should conduct a self-assessment of your marketability and value in your current position so that you can figure out just what you need to do to increase your marketability. Perhaps you need to get an advanced degree, additional training, familiarize yourself with your industry's trade publications, join a professional association or enter a new market all together. The key here is to brainstorm all the possible ways that you can increase your knowledge and skill base in order to bring additional value to any company that you choose to work for.

Taking time to assess your marketability, allows you to work on the skills and qualities that will enable you to move forward and work at the higher paying ends of your industry. In addition to assessing your marketability, learn how to become an indispensable asset to your boss and your company. To do this get a clear sense of what people in the top decision making positions want and need. Then, make it your mission to deliver it.

1. What are two things that you can do by the end of this month to increase your market value?
2. What have you learned recently that can be applied on the job to improve your performance and increase productivity?
3. What are the required skills and expertise necessary for advancement and higher pay in your industry?

Motivational Morsel #21.
Build Your Brand

If you look at the truly successfully people at work and in the business world, you will notice one common thread. They are adept at distinguishing themselves from the crowd by communicating their values, personality and abilities through the work that they do. In essence, they are skilled at building their brand. I often hear women down play the importance of branding or who say that branding is only for mega corporations like: Volvo, Gerber or Xerox. But in today's competitive marketplace the reality is, whether you are the front desk receptionist, a middle manager or the CEO, branding is an essential skill that will enable you to stand out from the crowd and stay employed for as long as you choose to be. Branding is not about being braggadocios. It's about putting the most positive and memorable spin on the work that you do in order to make a lasting impression.

One of the most damaging things that women do to kill their brand is minimize the importance of the work that they do. How many times have you asked a girlfriend or female co-worker to describe what she does only to have her respond with a self-diminishing answer like: "I'm just a supervisor." When was the last time you heard a man minimize the importance of his position? In fact, more often than not, men will make their jobs sound like the most important job in the company, no matter where they reside on the organization chart. We can take a lesson from men in this regard.

Remember every job is critical to helping a company achieve it's plans and goals, from the custodian or security officer who keeps the building clean and safe to the top level executive who goes out and raises the capital. So don't minimize the importance of the work that you do. With this in mind, here are 5 tips to help you build your brand.

1. Spend some time thinking about what distinguishes you from others that do what you do. What unique skills, talents and abilities do you bring to your work that make you stand out from the crowd?
2. Make a list of three to five things that you do well and that bring you the most satisfaction at work. Zeroing in on these things will help you to begin building your brand.
3. Keep a record of your achievements and accomplishments, both big and small. Review it regularly to gain information about what you do often and what you do well.
4. Stay current on developments in your industry by reading books, trade journals and taking workshops.
5. Get in the habit of introducing yourself by way of a 60 second elevator speech: For example, you could say something like: *I am the Program Director for a nonprofit agency where I am responsible for ensuring that parents who are at risk for losing their children, get the training and services they need to keep their families in tact.*

Chapter 4.
Letting Go Of The Ledge

Motivational Morsel #22.
Get Out of Your Comfort Zone

In my book, *The Single Mom's Little Book of Wisdom*, I discuss the importance of getting out of your comfort zone. I believe it merits repeating here. So here goes............

If you want to achieve radical results, you've got to do something that you've never done before – something that stretches you, forces you to grow, builds your skills, pulls out your potential and challenges you to rise to higher heights. And whatever do, you cannot allow fear to hold your back.

Far too often, fear is the only thing that stands in the way of you and your dreams. We come into this world with only two fears: the fear of falling and the fear of loud noises. All other fears are learned responses.

Fear is one of the most dangerous time bandits. Why? Because fear discourages you from pursuing your dreams, trying new things and it causes you to stay in situations that you have outgrown. Whenever you feel fearful of trying something new or difficult remind yourself that you have what it takes to make it. If that doesn't work, feel the fear and do it anyway. What have you got to lose? Today, take the plunge and get out of your comfort zone.

Motivational Morsel #23.
Just Do It

Everyone knows the famous Nike slogan that goes: *Just do it*! These are three simple words that pack a lot of power. Why? Because implicit in this statement is: *Have a little faith and take action now.* No excuses! No more deliberating! No more pondering over it!

Many people who are thought of as overnight successes, simply made up their minds to take action, even if they couldn't see the whole picture from beginning to end. They simply acted on their ideas and learned what they needed to learn as they went along. They got started on their plans and dreams with the information and resources they had on hand. They didn't wait for the perfect opportunity to arise or until they had all their ducks lined up in a row. They just went out and did what they had to do.

So often we don't act on our dreams because we focus on the roadblocks, on what we do not have, instead of taking stock of what we do have. You are already equipped with everything you need to succeed. As Mary Kay Ash, said, *"When you come to a roadblock, take a detour."* When you cannot move forward, move sideways, go in through the backdoor or maneuver around it. The lesson here is to just keep moving.

Today, pick an area of your life that you want to work on, be it: financial, career, relationships, or health and just do it.

1. Where in your life could it be said that you need to just do it?
2. Are you feeling intimidated because you don't have all the pieces pulled together yet? If so, what are you going to do to push past your doubts and fears?

3. A powerful strategy that many successful people employ is the rule of 5. The rule of 5 is doing five things each day, or if that feels too overwhelming, each week to move you in the direction of your goals. With this in mind, What 5 things can you do today or this week to move you in the direction of your goals? Write it down and just do it.

Motivational Morsel #24.
Act As If

In the movie, "Six Degrees of Separation" Will Smith plays a character who impersonates Sydney Poitier's son and goes around riding on his "father's celebrity status" in order to gain access to wealth, resources and influential people. He acted the part of a famous person's son in order to live the life that he desired. While I do not advocate impersonating other people, the lesson I take from Will Smith's character is you've got to act the part before you can play the part. This means thinking, talking, behaving, dressing and feeling like the person you want to become. When you act the part, you set a course of action in motion for the right people, resources and situations to come your way.

In the late 90's I attended a seminar given by New York Times best-selling author and international life coach, Iyanla Vanzant. After hearing her speak and reading her books, I knew that I wanted to speak and write for a living too. I asked myself: what did I have to do to become a professional speaker and author? I read books on speaking and writing. I bought audio and video learning programs. I took a business course to learn how to set up my business. I attended workshop and seminars.

Then, I decided to set up shop and act the part of a professional speaker and author. I upgraded my wardrobe. Had business cards made. Called every company, organization and association that I could think of and made my sales pitch. I got a lot of rejection. Some people were downright rude. Others hung up on me in mid sentence. But, no matter what challenges I faced, I refused to give up. Why? Because I was serious about my goal. I kept making calls and sending out brochures, until one day somebody hired me to speak. And the rest is history.

Once I decided to act the part and not allow anything to stop me, I achieved my goal of becoming a professional speaker and author. And the same thing goes for you. If you start to act the part, you will eventually attract the resources you need to play the part.

- The purpose of acting the part is to program your mind and emotions to develop the kinds of skills, habits and characteristics that fall in line with the life style you want to attain and the type of person you want to become. With this in mind, what areas in your life do you need to act the part in order to position yourself to play the part?
- How do you think your life would change if you started to develop the kinds of habits and characteristics that are consistent with the kind of person you want to become?

Motivational Morsel #25.
If It's Happening To You, It's Happening For You

When obstacles and challenges show up in our lives, the first thing we do is resist and ask: Why me? Our bodies tense up. Our thoughts becomes scattered. We become fearful, and we exert the majority of our time and energy talking about how bad our problems are rather than see the experience for what it is: a test, a lesson in resiliency and an opportunity to learn and grow.

Always remember that the most difficult experiences and the toughest obstacles often teach you the most powerful lessons like: Faith, forgiveness, patience, resourcefulness, and empathy. When we resist life's challenges, we run the risk of missing important life lessons that are necessary for us to get to the next level and fulfill our life's purpose. Challenges and setbacks are a continual part of life. They are your daily testing ground. Depending on how you handle them, they either become your stumbling blocks or your steps to success. When adversity comes your way, instead of asking: *Why is this happening to me?* Ask: *Why is this happening for me?*

1. Think about a particularly difficult challenge you've had. What lesson might life be trying to teach you through this experience?
2. Sometimes adversity comes in our life to teach us something about ourselves. With this in mind, what do you stand for? What principle, cause or value would you defend to the death? What would you find a way to do no matter what?
3. When adversity strikes, we always have resources in our arsenal that we can pull from that give us small victories, moments of clarity and blessed assurance. It may not seem like it, but we do. We have faith, integrity, discipline, friends, family and so on. What resources can you draw from as you go through your valley experience?

51

Motivational Morsel #26.
Be Willing To Let Go

The story is told of a mountain climber who was almost at the top of the mountain when he lost his footing and started to swiftly slide down toward the river. Just before he was about to fall in, he grabs hold of the ledge and hangs there, with his feet dangling in mid air a few inches above the raging waters.

In a panic he cries out, *Lord please help me.* God answers, *"I'll help you, but first you must let go of the ledge."* He replies, *Lord I can't let go of the ledge: The current is too strong, I don't have the proper landing gear and my equipment is not equipped for that type of fall.* The Lord replies: *Whenever you're ready to let go, I'll be here to catch you.*

There's a price we must pay to get to the next level. That price is called letting go – letting go of where we are in order to get where we need to go. Holding on to the security of what's familiar and comfortable, prevents you from stepping boldly into your future. The security blankets in our lives come in many forms like: jobs we hate that pay the bills, emotionally draining relationships, habits that no longer serve us well, business relationships that no longer fit where we are or any thing else that stunts our growth. While security blankets offer the illusion of safety, the truth is they only hold us back.

Letting go is the most powerful expression of faith because it forces you to move forward even though you don't know for certain what the outcome will be. It's about trusting God and trusting the process so that you can walk in the fullness of your potential and live your best life.

Every successful person I have met or read about, at some point had to let go of the very thing they thought they could not function without. And that very act of letting go was the catalyst that set everything else in motion for them to go to their place of destiny.

Whether you choose to let go now or in the future, one thing is certain, each day that you continue to hold on to the things that hold you back, you keep yourself from realizing all of your ambitions. So today, take a deep breath, call upon your faith and with both hands let go of the things that keep you bound.

1. Where can it be said in your life that you need to let go? What are you going to do about it?
2. What do you think will happen if you let go? Will you be better off in the long run?
3. What great things might await you if you stepped out on faith and boldly let go of the ledge?

Motivational Morsel #27.
It's OK If You Dance To A Different Beat

At a very early age, we are taught to fit the mold, color inside the lines and get on board with the masses. But sometimes the masses are asses and when you find yourself in the midst of asinine people, you've got to find another crowd and do what you've got to do to stay true to yourself. People have had opinions about other people since the beginning of time and will continue to judge and talk about those who do their own thing in their own unique way. Don't worry about the people who don't get you. They're not supposed to get you because your destiny is not connected to theirs. Just keep doing the things that you feel called to do and the rest will work itself out.

If you really think about it, it's futile to obsess over what other people think. There was a time when people thought the world was flat and those who knew it was round were ridiculed. There was a time when people thought the sun revolved around the earth and to state otherwise would put you at risk for public humiliation. So as you can see just because the majority of people see things a particular way doesn't make their perspective right and your perspective wrong. It just means that you have a difference of opinion. So do your own thing in your own way and don't worry if your music plays out a little differently.

- Are you obsessing over what other people think? If so, why are you allowing what other people think to take up so much of your headspace?
- What's the worst that people would say if you began to live at loud? Now that you know, prepare yourself and live out loud anyway.

Motivational Morsel #28.
Sometimes Courage Comes In Small Doses

Contrary to popular belief, courage is not the absence of fear. It is doing what you have to do in spite of your fears. Courage is doing the very thing that you're afraid to do with knees trembling, knots in your stomach and everything inside of you kicking, screaming and begging you to run in the opposite direction. Having courage is about turning challenges into opportunities, failures into fresh starts and pain and misery into your area of ministry.

The reason we don't realize how courageous we truly are is because oftentimes courage comes in small doses like: setting boundaries with an overbearing person, advocating for your children, walking away from a bad relationship that you've invested a lot of time in or achieving a long lost goal that you never thought you would achieve. These seemingly small acts of brevity are the real measure of true courage.

However, courage is not limited to just doing something new. It also means being willing to become someone new. Some people may act fearlessly on the outside and present a bold public persona, but when you look a little closer you see that they're afraid to do the internal work that requires one to look deep within and examine one's beliefs.

So today, I invite you to live more courageously and acknowledge the small acts of brevity that lead to a life well lived.

- Name three courageous things you've done over the past year. What small doses of courage have you been called to unleash?
- Write down five things that you would do if you were ten times bolder. Pick one and do it this week.

Chapter 5.
Breaking The Habit of
Self-Sabotage

Motivational Morsel #29.
Identify The Things That Stand Between You and Your Greatness

Ninety percent of the things that stand between you and your greatness are within your control. Only a small percentage has to do with something outside of you. As hard as this may be to accept, nobody but you can stand in your way. Even if other people close a few doors, refuse to share their resources, keep you out of their little circle, or the cards are stacked against you, you are the only one who stands between you and your greatness. Why? Because while success is something that you achieve, greatness is who you are. Far too often when our lives do not work out the way we plan, we blame other people and make them responsible for our success and happiness.

Always remember that no matter what has happened to you, how much it hurts or how badly you feel about it, if you want your life to change for the better, then you have to be the one to change things. Change may look like a change in attitude or asking for the resources you need or letting go of what's familiar so that you can move on to bigger and better things. No matter what your change looks like, it's up to you to change the things in your life that need to be changed.

What are the things that stand between you and your greatness and what do you intend to do about it? Once you have determined the things that stand between you and your greatness, the next step is to commit to a plan of self-improvement. There are several ways that you can improve yourself. One way is to read books that motivate you and inspire you to greatness.

Another is to make up your mind to eliminate the habits that do not serve you well so that you can adopt new habits that are more in line with where you want to be and the type of person you want to become.

The lesson here is if you find that your beliefs, attitude and practices are no longer working for you, then you must make the necessary changes to achieve a different result.

When we find that what we are doing does not make us feel good and does not bring us the results we want, then we must stop doing the things that no longer work. Today, take a long, hard look at yourself and eliminate the things that stand between you and your greatness.

- Is there anything that you are doing to block your blessings or sabotage yourself?
- Are there any long-standing beliefs, attitudes or habits that you need to change?
- Make a commitment to yourself to work on one area of self-improvement this week.

Motivational Morsel #30.
Never Confuse Your Circumstances With The Truth Of Who You Are

You may not own your own home, a car or have impressive credentials that follow your last name. You may not have any appreciating assets, or an emergency fund that you can draw from in the event that the stuff hits the fan. You may depend on the government for your food and shelter, or be so knee-deep in debt that the little money you do have is taken out of your check before you have a chance to see it. But no matter what your situation, never confuse your circumstances with the truth of who you are.

Sometimes when our lives play out differently than we anticipate, we have a tendency to beat up on ourselves for not being where we thought we ought to be. Try not to should on yourself. Always remember that no matter where you are, you can make progress. There are golden opportunities all around you to see things a new way, try a new thing and make a fresh start. Instead of allowing yourself to sink into depression, ask yourself: How can I grow from this experience and use it for my betterment? Knowing what I now know, what do I need to do in order to move forward?

Unfortunately, many people allow temporary setbacks and faith-testing circumstances to knock them off their path and cause them to give up all hope. Don't sabotage yourself this way. Your circumstances can change on a dime, but the truth is always constant. You were created in an image of love and light with an inborn knowledge of everything you need to live richly. It is during the testing times that life calls on you to draw from your internal well so that you can keep moving forward, no matter what.

Today, count your blessings. Take stock of what you do have. Then turn your circumstances into a blank check and write yourself a brand new perspective on life.

59

Motivational Morsel # 31.
Feeling Down Is One Thing,
Staying There Is Another

As hard as this may be to accept, there are times in our lives when we choose to stay in our pain. We keep telling the same sad story, listening to the same sad song, sitting in the same sad spot, wearing the same old, sad looking clothes. Then we wonder why we can't stop crying and why the intensity of the pain seems like it will never, ever end.

Bad things are going to happen. Bad things are going to happen to good people. Painful, life-altering events are going to occur. There's no way around it. That's the price we pay for living. And when painful life events occur, it is critical that we take the time needed to grieve. Grieving is a necessary and natural part of the healing process. But there's a fine line between going through the grieving process and staying in your pain. Grieving is the process of going through a series of progressive emotional stages that eventually lead you to a place of acceptance. Staying in your pain is about checking out emotionally, giving up on life and refusing to do the simple things that make each day a little easier to bear.

In the midst of painful life experiences it is normal and natural to focus on how bad you feel, how much you hurt and how much you long for things to be the way they used to be. You have a right to grieve. You've got a right to cry. To yell and scream in the privacy of your home. You have the right to stay under the covers, eat as much ice cream as you want and to mentally tell the whole world... *to go to hell...* You have the right to do all of these things...for a season. But at some point, if you plan on functioning among the living, you will have to find a way to start picking up the pieces so that you can come out of your pain.

Take things one day at a time, one hour at a time or in fifteen-minute increments if that is all that you can do. But at some point come up for air, take the funky clothes off, stop listening to songs that depress you, stop calling in sick and put the ice cream down. You are not going to feel better by way of osmosis. You've got to do something to make yourself feel better. Do something each day that lifts you up a little until you can come to a place where you can finally face life head on.

Here are five simple rules that should help you behave your way into feeling better.

1. Do not go more than two days with showering and combing your hair. You get to lay around in a funk for the equivalent of one weekend, but come Monday morning, start the day off fresh.
2. Do not play any sad songs for more than one hour at a time.
3. Do not go more than 24 hours without answering your phone. Let at least one person know that you are still alive.
4. Lean on friends and family. Yes, they've heard your story a thousand times but if you can't turn to your friends and family, who can you turn to.
5. Do one small thing each day that makes you feel a little better. Take a walk. Watch a funny movie. Buy a new pair of shoes. Better yet, go window shopping and put the shoe money into your 401K Plan.

Motivational Morsel #32.
Don't Let The Past Keep You From Moving Forward

Negative past experiences can adversely affect you for the rest of your life, if you do not make the choice to come to terms with your past. Some of us are born into dysfunctional families, while others experience drama and trauma along the way. But, no matter what has happened to you, or what other people have done, you cannot allow your past to keep you from moving forward.

Far too often, people carry around unresolved feelings of anger, hurt and resentment. These feeling can grown inside of you like a cancer and make you look at life through a terminally ill lens. When negative unresolved feelings take over, you can become so accustomed to negativity that you leave no room for the good to come in. Walking through life this way keeps you from seeing past your feelings and circumstances. Not to mention, it keeps you stagnant.

I'm not saying that your situation isn't challenging or that life always plays fair. What I am saying is if you continue to allow your past to color your future, you'll stay stuck in a place of powerlessness and victimization. And you've got too much living to do to allow your past to keep you in captivity. Today, work on yourself, call a therapist or join a support group and make the decision to put the past behind you.

Motivational Morsel #33.
Don't Sweat The Small Stuff,
Especially Small People

Why is it that so many of us focus our time and energy on people and things that really don't matter? We live in a fast-paced, stressful world. We compound that level of stress when we sweat trivial things and trivial people. What's important to realize is when you get bent out of shape over the little things, become easily irritated or overact over the tiniest, little, annoyances, you are the one who becomes stressed out and upset. When you lose control and get puffed up over things that really don't matter, you waist precious energy that could be better spent doing the things that bring you joy.

In short, sweating the small stuff while trying to bring your plans and goals into fruition is an act of self-sabotage. Because your own actions and frustrations will derail your success. When you stop sweating the small stuff, you become more purpose-driven and focused. Life's little annoyances won't go away, but they won't get to you as often either. Today, think bigger and be bigger. Leave no space in your heart or head for small-minded people and their trivial ways.

Motivational Morsel #34.
Become The Landlord Of Your Mind

The single most important thing that you can do to feel good about yourself and keep a positive outlook on life is, take control of your thoughts. While you cannot control every thought that comes into your mind, you can certainly choose not to dwell on the negative ones. This is what I call, treating your mind like an apartment.

When you treat your mind like an apartment you become the landlord and your thoughts become the tenants. And as the landlord of your mind, whenever you have a tenant who is not paying rent (a negative thought) it is up to you to evict that thought. What's important for you to realize is anything that you believe with certainty eventually becomes your reality, even if your beliefs are not consistent with your reality. Because you believe them to be true, they will be true for you. This is why it is so important that you monitor the internal dialogue that goes on inside your head and that you make every effort to allow the voice of confidence to become louder than the voice of doubt and insecurity. Here's how:

Try to identify the negative thoughts that are preventing you from living your best life. Once you have identified these thoughts, replace them with more positive self-affirming ones. For example, if you find yourself saying things like: *I'm broke.* Replace that chain of thought with: *I am actively seeking ways to increase my avenues for income.* If you find yourself saying things like: *I'll never find anyone great to share my life with.* Replace that chain of thought with: *There are wonderful people all around me, who could possibly be my potential mate. If I widen my mate selection pool and put myself out there more often, I will eventually meet someone who could be "The One."*

It goes without saying that: Your mind is the tool that creates your world. And the funny thing about tools are they can be used in two ways: to build or to tear down. So the next time you allow negative thoughts to run rampant in your head: Ask yourself: *Am I using my tool to build or tear down?*

Motivational Morsel #35.
If You Happen To Fall Down, Grab Hold of Something Sturdy and Get Back Up

Have you ever watched a toddler learning to walk? What happens? They take a few steps and fall. Sometimes they bump into things. Sometimes they hit their heads and stub their toes. And sometimes they collapse or completely fall on their backsides. But no matter how many times they fall down, bump their hands or have unforeseen objects tumble down on them, they keep getting up until they are able to steady themselves and walk.

There is no circumstance around you more powerful than the power that lies within you. When life knocks you down, you must call upon your toddler powers – your powers of determination, perseverance and sheer will power so that you can steady yourself and get back up.

It is the will to try and try again that enables you to keep moving even when the odds are stacked against you. And the longer you persist, the more determined you will become to get where you need to go. So when life knocks you down, remember your toddler powers and apply the five rules of toddler hood to help you keep on walking.

1. Grab hold of something sturdy.
2. See your way clear across the room.
3. Focus on you focal point.
4. If you fall down, bump your head, bust your lip or if unforeseen objects try to block your path, cry out for help.
5. Then, get up and keep on walking.

Chapter 6.
Taking Steps Towards Healthier Relationships

Motivational Morsel #36.
How People Come Into Your Life, Usually Determines How They Stay There

When Nancy met Charlie, he was in between jobs. He got fired from one and was supposedly looking for another. Charlie was cute. A good conversationalist. Seemed nice enough. And the sex was good to the bone. So when Charlie told Nancy that he had no place to live and no steady income coming in, Nancy suggested that he move in with her until he was able to get back on his feet.

Nancy had a good job at an insurance firm, a two-family home with paying tenants and a nice little nest egg she was saving for retirement. Charlie had his good looks and a size thirteen shoe.

Charlie has been living with Nancy for eight months and it doesn't seem like he's even trying to look for work. Nancy goes to work every day, pays all the bills. Then comes home to cook for Charlie. Lately, Nancy has been strapped for cash. She's been borrowing against her retirement fund to keep up with her rising expenses. Charlie is just happy to have a free ride.

It's important to keep in mind that all relationships are like silent contractual agreements. One party agrees to certain terms, provided the other party agrees to a few others. The problem comes in when the participating parties ignore the fine-print issues or believe that they can re-negotiate the terms after they've already signed on the dotted line.

What are the fine-print issues in your relationships? The things you failed to address, pretended not to notice and refused to bring to the surface. Did you say that certain characteristics did not bother you when they did? Did you put up with behaviors and attitudes that were diametrically opposed to your positive development? Did you sell yourself a dream when the truth of the matter was staring you smack in the face?

Did you remain in situations that broke you down as a woman and made your life more painful and dysfunctional than it had to be? See, you've got to know what the fine-print issues are, because it's the unspoken things and the underlying motives that almost always, break the deal.

If you want to be a sugar mama: be level headed about it. It's your money. You can do whatever you want with it. Just make sure to protect your assets. If you want to be a kept woman and trade your services for his goods: call it what it is. Don't call it a relationship when it's really a mutually beneficial arrangement...with a timeline. If you need a little maintenance while you're waiting on Mr. Right, don't confuse a regularly scheduled tune up with love and commitment. If you do, you are setting yourself up for heartache. And please be smart enough not to move the maintenance man in. If the man you long for is committed to someone else and comes by every now and then when he's able to fit you in, understand that you're giving your power away, no matter how unemotional and detached you think you can be.

It's your life. It's your body. It's your heart. And what you do with these things is your business. You're a grown woman. But also be grown enough to tell yourself the truth, all the time, in all situations.

As the saying goes: How people come into your life, usually determines how they stay there. So pay close attention to how and when people show up. Do they show up with carry on luggage and a closed heart? Or, do they show up in love and light ready and able to build and grow?

The best way to identify the fine-print issues in your relationships is to go over all of the details with a fine-tooth comb, pay close attention to how you feel as well as how the other person responds. Then, slow down long enough to read between the lines.

Motivational Morsel #37
There Are Some People You've Got To Love From A Distance

Rita and Lynne were childhood friends. They shared special secrets. Saw each other through first kisses, first crushes and first periods. They leaned on one another during the tough times. They attended the same college. Majored in the same subject. And as luck would have it they got married around the same time. Rita and Lynne made a promise to one another that they would always be friends to the end.

Rita got a job at a local newspaper. Lynne worked as a manager for a mega mall. Rita's career started to quickly take off. She went from writing for the local newspaper to landing a senior editorial job for a major fashion magazine. Rita was traveling all over the world, hobnobbing with celebrities and gaining notoriety as a major player in the fashion world.

Whenever Rita, and Lynne got together, Lynne criticized Rita about her latest article, told her how bad she looked, and teased her about the twenty pounds she gained. If fact, whenever Lynne saw Rita she had something negative to say. Rita found herself becoming more and more self-conscious and doubtful. Lynne was becoming openly hostile and resentful. When Rita confronted Lynne about her behavior, Lynne told Rita to stop being so sensitive and take it all in stride. Rita dropped the subject and continued her friendship with Lynne. But each time they got together, Rita felt like a piece of her self-esteem was being chipped away.

Far too often we stay in relationships that we have outgrown out of a false sense of loyalty. Or we tolerate insulting behavior out of the need to prove that we're still the same old person and that nothing has really changed.

But people do change. Friends sometimes outgrow each other or take different routes. And, sometimes when your life takes a different turn and you have nothing in common anymore it's time to say your goodbyes and keep things moving. When people mistreat you, whether subtly or overtly, it is up to you to set the boundary, even if it means putting a little distance between you and the other person.

If your relationships are not supportive or helping you to grow, then they are keeping you stagnant or bringing you down. There is no middle ground here.

Most of us reject this idea because we find it hard to believe that sometimes the very people who claim to love us and who call themselves our friends, can be the very same people who cannot handle our growth or who simply do not have our best interests in mind.

When the people who claim to care about you use and abuse you, play psychological head games, dismiss you or cause you undue stress and drama, it's time to draw your lines in the sand and love them from a distance.

Motivational Morsel #38
When People Show You Who They Are,
Believe Them

Tanya was coming off of a two-year hiatus. She was healing from a relationship that ended very badly. She was vulnerable, wounded and looking for validation.

Tanya had been around the block a few times. She had two ex-husbands, a baby's daddy, four children in the mix and an ex-boyfriend she called on from time to time when she was in between relationships and needed a little tune up.

Mike was not looking for a relationship when he met Tanya, but was he open to becoming friends with benefits. They started talking and found that they had similar issues and interests. Tanya was lonely, in need of companionship and quite attracted to him. Actually, the attraction was mutual. They talked about their plans and dreams. Talked about how difficult it was to meet good people. Then, they talked about all the sexual things they wanted to do to each other. Two months later Mike had his own dresser draw, a toothbrush in the cup holder and his voice was the greeting you heard when you called Tanya's residence and got her answering machine.

After five years of living together, Tanya gently approached Mike about the subject of where the relationship was headed. She wanted to get married. Or, at least engaged with a pending wedding date. She was tired of playing house and thought it was time for the two of them to build a home. Mike reminded Tanya that he made it clear from day one that he did not want to get married or have any more children. Tanya thought in due time he would change.

A few months after the marriage conversation other women started calling the house, Mike started working more frequently. Coming in late. Showering before he went to bed. And lost all interest in sex. Then there were those brazen occasions when he didn't come home at all. But Tanya hung in there. Never said a word. She was intent on building a home with him. Hoping that if she hung in there long enough, his behavior would change.

Then right before they were scheduled to go to a family cookout, Mike told Tanya that he had met someone else, and would be moving out by the end of the week.

When people show you who they are, believe them. Truth be told, most people show you who they are within the first few minutes of meeting them. It is up to you to pay attention. When you meet an individual and they make their intentions known, either by way of their words, actions, or the things they don't say, you've got enough data to make an intelligent decision. You owe it to yourself, not to go through your relationships with mental blinders on your eyes and emotional earplugs in your ears.

Motivational Morsel #39.
There Are Some Situations That We Innocently Fall Into and Others Where The Writing Is On The Wall

Patti was in the midst of transition. She was recovering from one unhealthy relationship and entering into another. Her ex was abusive and controlling. Her new beau was laid back and easygoing. Sensitive and kind.

Patti promised herself that she would never let another man abuse or control her again. So she put up ironclad walls and enclosed a fortress around her heart. Patti was heavily guarded, so much so, that if a man showed the slightest bit of interest she would shut him down immediately and go into her routine about how strong and independent she was and that the only thing a man would do right now was get in her way or throw her off her game.

Then he showed up...laid back, cool and composed. No pressure. No promises. In fact, he didn't even come at her sexually. So she felt safe enough to let down her guard. Patti knew how to handle sexually suggestive men and put them in their place. She knew how to use her feminine wit and social savvy to keep men at bay. Patti was an attractive woman, so she was used to being hit on all the time.

But he was different, or seemed like it on the surface. He asked her about her plans and dreams. Got her to open up emotionally. And the more he got inside her head, the more Patti let down her guard. Patti liked being around him. She enjoyed their conversation. She felt emotionally safe. The chemistry was strong. The vibe was comfortable and easy. And the sexual attraction was becoming too much to bear. She found herself thinking about him often and wondering what it would be like to be held by him, to touch him, to make slow, passionate love.

There was just one problem: *He was married with two children and Patti was slowly starting to fall in love.*

He never lied to her about his situation. In fact, he even talked to her about his wife. They told themselves that there was nothing wrong with just being friends. Besides, Patti always thought that she was the kind of woman who would never cross the line. But loneliness mixed with sexual yearning have a funny way of having a mind of their own.

The affair was brief and all consuming. Both of them walked away angry, regretful and wounded. And what started out as a casual conversation between two people with unmet needs and unfulfilled desires, turned into an all out, full-fledged affair.

There are some situations that we innocently fall into and others where the writing is on the wall. All of the warning signs are present and the red flags are in full view, but we jump full speed ahead tossing common sense aside and throwing caution to the wind. Or, we tell ourselves that we can handle a little, taste of temptation without opening the door to heartache and pain.

Always remember that you cannot play with fire without getting burnt. And you cannot lay in the mud without running the risk of getting soiled. There's a price we pay when we ignore important signposts. That price is unwanted drama, avoidable pain and a question mark around our character.

When you find yourself in red flag situations, you must do your best to heed the warning signs and look for a way out. Pay attention, because there is always a way out. Pay attention to your common sense, your God Sense and the potential ramifications that your behavior might bring. Attention must be paid; otherwise you will continually find yourself in situations that dishonor you, demean you as a woman and that can have devastating effects on innocent people who did not asked to be dragged into your mess.

The bottom and top line is, when the writing is on the wall, it is your responsibility to take heed to it.

Motivational Morsel # 40.
If Real Love Showed Up, Would You Be Ready?

Some of us are so addicted to dysfunction and drama, that we're not able to appreciate a good thing until it's gone.

There isn't a day that goes by that Martha doesn't regret that she didn't try harder to make a go of her marriage. Her ex-husband Joe was a good man. Gentle, sensitive and kind. He had a quiet way about him. He was not a man of many words. But when he spoke he usually had something pensive and profound to say. Joe practically worshiped the ground Martha walked on. He worked hard, paid the bills on time and did the little things like bringing Martha flowers and candy in order to show her how much she was loved.

But Martha had a thing for bad boys. She thrived on the thrill of the chase. A history of abuse and abandonment had warped her outlook on love and caused her to continually get into relationships with abusive and unavailable men.

Martha didn't like herself very much, but she was too psychologically scarred to know it. She had all the outer trappings of success: a high paying job, a fabulous home, impressive credentials and a 401K plan with appreciating stocks and bonds. On the outside, it seemed like she was healthy and ready. But on the inside Martha was broken and torn.

The reason some of us cannot find a good man is not because all the good men are already taken. It's because some of us are not emotionally ready to have adult relationships based on mutual support and growth. Granted, there are many men who play the field and treat women as commodities to conquer. But there is also a whole nother pool of men who are honest and who want to build and grow with a good woman.

However, some of us have been swimming in the emotional cesspool for so long that we still wear the residue from past pain and drama.

The spiritual law of attraction states: *What you draw to you is what you are*. Like energy attracts like energy. Have you ever noticed that needy women almost always attract emotionally unavailable men? And controlling, self-righteous women always attract men who can't seem to do anything right. And women who feel badly about themselves usually end up with men who reinforce their negative beliefs.

So if you keep attracting the same kind of men, it probably means you are the same kind of woman. The law of attraction is always at work, whether you believe in it or not. And we are either attracting positive experiences into our lives or repelling them. This is why it is so important that you put in the work to make yourself happier, healthier and whole.

You owe it to yourself to live your best life. A large part of living your best life is becoming healthy and whole enough to sustain healthy relationships. So before you rush out and get back out there again, take some time to work on yourself, get your priorities in order and become the kind of person you want to attract. This way when real love shows up, you'll be 100% ready to receive it.

Motivational Morsel #41.
If You Want To Know Why Your Life Is Filled With Dysfunction and Drama Go Back To The Beginning

When Betty was a little girl, her father left her mother. He went out for a pack of cigarettes and never came back. Betty's mother was young and attractive. She had a nice figure. So she never went for too long without the company of a willing and able man.

By the time Betty was twelve two of her mother's boyfriends molested her and her youngest uncle had that hungry look in his eyes. At a young age Betty knew what men liked. By the time she was sixteen, she had two abortions, an STD and she was turning tricks for two different married men. Betty had her first child at seventeen and her third by twenty-one. Yes, Betty was on a mission to self-destruct. Now before you get indignant and judgmental and talk about how trifling Betty is...remember to go back to the beginning.

If you want to get to the root of a behavior, go back ...way back and you will find your answer. While your story may not be as devastating as Betty's, everybody comes with a little history.

Self-analysis is crucial to breaking self-defeating behavior patterns. A critical self-analysis allows you to look back over your life so that you can give special attention to the areas in your life that may need a little mending.

No matter what has happened to you or what kind of adversity you face, if you want to put an end to drama and trauma, you've got to look your issues straight in the eye and develop a plan for dealing with them. In the meantime, always remember that you are blessed, highly favored and worthy. And most of all, you don't have to prove yourself, give away your power, stay in situations that tear you down or sell yourself short in order to be loved.

Motivational Morsel #42.
Does He Love You Enough To Wipe Your Behind?

My grandmother, Elsie Lee Daglow, was one of the wisest women I knew. She grew up in a small town in South Hill, Virginia in the 1920's and came to New York in search of a better life. My grandmother came from good stock – generations of strong women who did what they had to do to survive and create a better life for their children. My grandmother was married twice and had ten children. Seven that she gave birth to and three that she inherited from her second husband. She didn't have much money, but she was rich beyond measure.

Before she died, we would have long talks around the kitchen table. She'd be frying chicken or making sweet potato biscuits, while I helped and tried to soak up her love and wisdom. As we broached the subject of love, she said: *Before you give your heart to a man, make sure he loves you enough to wipe your behind?* After being thoroughly mortified by the images that came to mind, I tried to take in what my grandmother was really saying and asked her to explain exactly what she meant. She said: *When you are young and naïve, you're concerned with flowers, candy and getting butterflies in your stomach when he walks into the room. But as you have children and get older those things become less important and it's really about the character of a man, the way he cares for you and stands by you when the chips are down. Everyday ain't going to be a party. But at the end of the day, do you trust him to stick with you when things get rough and ugly, to care for you in the dirtiest places? That's real love, the kind that you can count on when you're sick, frail, not as pretty as you used to be, if you ever get into an accident that robs you of your independence and mobility, when you're broke, broken and when life beats you down. See baby, love is not a feeling. It is choosing to be good to the one you claim to love.*

So in the words of my wise old grandmother: When you meet a man who you believe could be the one, ask yourself, *Does he love me enough to wipe my behind?*

Conclusion

As we come to the end of this book, I feel a tremendous sense of gratitude that you choose *The Busy Woman's Little Book of Motivation* as the catalyst to spark something new in you. My prayer is that you are on your way to becoming a woman of possibility, a woman of action...and a woman who lives life fully.

My goal in writing this book has been to help women approach their lives from a position of empowerment and to embrace all the wonderful things that life has to offer. After all, we only come through once.

Keep looking for ways to own your power. Don't be afraid to let go of the ledge. And have the audacity to go after the things you want in life. See you on the path...

Book Discussion Guide

The discussion questions in this section are designed to get you talking and thinking about what you can do to feel more empowered in a tangible way and replenish yourself when life starts to feel overwhelming. Get together with a group of women and initiate a discussion around the questions and themes presented in this book.

1. In Motivational Morsel #1. *Decide What You Want and Have The Audacity To Go After It*, the author says that most people who have the audacity to go after the things they want out of life usually end up getting them. Do you agree with this statement? Why or why not? What does audacity mean to you? Are you audacious? What do you think prevents people, particularly women, from being audacious enough to go after the things they want out of life? When you think of women who have audacity, what names come to mind? How can you borrow from their boldness to become unstoppable and undeterred?

2. Do you think that women give themselves enough credit and acknowledge their successes both big and small? In Motivational Morsel #2. *Honor The Life You Have Now*, the author says that far too many women treat their lives like a dress rehearsal putting their plans and dreams on hold. Why do you think so many women do this to themselves? Why do we hold ourselves back from living our fullest, most rewarding lives? Where do we get our ideas about how women ought to be in the world? What can we as women do to honor ourselves and our lives more fully?

3. In Motivational Morsel #6. *Be Your Own Cheerleader*, the author talks about the importance of encouraging yourself and talking to yourself   as if you were talking to

a star athlete. What can we as women do to change our scripts from one of self-doubt to one of self-encouragement? What daily things can we do to love ourselves unconditionally and feel more positively about who we are and what we bring to the world? What affirmations, scriptures or positive statements help you to feel encouraged? What keeps you centered and hopeful, especially during the tough times in your life?

4. In Motivational Morsel #7. *Get Out Of Your Own Way,* the author says that every dream you have and every goal you set is a preview of what's possible. What are your dreams and goals telling you about what's possible for you? Are you holding yourself back in any way? Are you sure? If you are holding yourself back, what can you do to get out of your own way?

5. How important is it that women take time for themselves? Do some women take the superwoman act too far? Is there a difference between a strong woman and a woman of strength? What's the difference? In Motivational Morsel #8. *Even Superwoman Had To Take Off Her Cape,* the author says that many of us are at the point where we are overwhelmed and overextended because we take on too much and try to be too many things to too many people. Do you think this is true of women in general? What can we as women do to cup the cup full enough to feed ourselves?

6. In Motivational Morsel #11. *Identify What's Draining You,* the author says that as women we've got to be vigilant at noticing the energy drains in our lives so that we can become more productive and effective. What kinds of things can drain a person's power and productivity, especially women? What can we as women do to become more vigilant about plugging the energy drains in our lives?

83

How important is balance? Can women have it all at the same time? What does having it all mean to you?

7. Do you believe that happiness is a feeling, a state of mind or both? What do you think is the key to being happy? Is there a difference between happiness and joy? Is it possible to have everything you want and still be unhappy? In Motivational Morsel #12. *The World Can't Give You Happiness and The World Can't Take It Away*, the author says that if we are to live happy and fulfilling lives, then we must make our happiness a personal priority. On a scale of 1 to 10 how much of a personal priority is your happiness to you? What are some simple things that women can do to make their happiness more of a personal priority? What will you do as of tomorrow to make your happiness a personal priority?

8. In Motivational Morsel #15. *Map Out A Plan for Learning, Growing and Advancing*, the author says that having a plan puts you in the driver's seat of your career. What are some effective ways for women to take charge of their careers? What kinds of things should be included in a strategic career plan? What are some of the effects of not having a strategic plan for learning, growing and advancing in your career? Do you have a strategic career plan? What's the plan?

9. Do you think that women support one another or sabotage each other in the workplace? What have your experiences been like with other women in the workplace? How can we as women be more supportive of each other in the workplace? In Motivational Morsel #16. *Make Office Politics Work for You*, the author says that becoming politically savvy is about learning how to navigate your company's political maze without compromising your core values.

What are the politics at your company? Are you able to navigate the political maze? What can you do to become more politically savvy while still remaining true to your core values?

10. In Motivational Morsel # 20. *Know Your Market Value*, the author says that many women give their ideas and services away too freely and we don't ask for perks and raises as often as we should. Do you agree? Why or why not? What can women do to increase their market value individually as well as collectively? In your opinion, what do women need to be sure to do in order to be well respected and well compensated for their time and talent?

11. In Motivational Morsel #21. *Build Your Brand*, the author says that one of the most damaging things that women do to kill their brand is minimize the work that they do. In what ways do women minimize themselves and their jobs? Why do you think that so many women confuse branding with being braggadocios? Are you adept at communicating your brand to others? If you had to introduce yourself and the skills and services you have to offer by way of a 60 second elevator speech, what would you say? What does your elevator speech say about your brand?

12. In Motivational Morsel #23. *Just Do It*, the author talks about the importance of practicing the rule of 5: 5 things each week or day that move you in the direction of your goals. With this in mind, what 5 things can you do either today or this week to move yourself one step closer to your goals? Why do you think so many people put off working towards their goals? What are some of the drawbacks of procrastination?

13. Letting go of the security blankets in our lives is difficult for even the most fearless of women? Why do you think it's so difficult to let go of the security blankets in our lives even when they keep us stuck or bring us down? In Motivational Morsel #26. *Be Willing To Let Go*, the author says the price we have to pay to get to the next level is letting go of where we are now. Do you think this is easier said than done? Is there anything in your life that you need to let go of that you are still holding on to? What do you think it will take for you to be able to let go?

14. In Motivational Morsel #28. *Sometimes Courage Comes In Small Doses*, the author defines courage as doing what you've got to do in spite of your fears. What does courage mean to you? Who are some of the courageous women you know and what makes them courageous in your eyes? What courageous things have you done in your life, even if they came in small doses? What can we as women do to live more courageously?

15. In Motivational Morsel # 33. *Don't Sweat The Small Stuff*, the author says that sweating the small stuff while trying to bring your goals and plans into fruition is a complete waste of time. If this is so, then why do so many of us sweat the small stuff, particularly small-minded people? In your opinion, what can we as women do to stop sweating the small stuff? What are some things that women can do to think and act more positively even in the midst of negative people?

16. Do you believe in the power of positive thinking? How do our thoughts affect our emotions and decisions? What are some of the consequences of negative thinking? In Motivational Morsel # 34. *Become The Landlord of Your*

Mind, the author talks about the importance of monitoring our mental dialogue and to let the voice of confidence ring louder than the voice of doubt and insecurity. Is this easier said than done? What are the benefits of this strategy? What can women do to become more positive in our thinking and actions? How can we pass this important lesson on to our daughters, sisters and girlfriends?

17. Negative past experiences can affect us for the rest of our lives if we don't make a conscious effort to make peace with the past. In Motivational Morsel # 32 *Don't Let The Past Keep You From Moving Forward,* the author stresses the importance of not allowing painful past events to keep you stuck and bitter. What are some of the ways that people allow themselves to be held captive by their past? Why does the past hold so much power for some? What can women do to move forward when they are struggling with unresolved issues from the past?

18. In Motivational Morsel #37. *There Are Some People You've Got To Love From A Distance,* the author states that far too often we remain in relationships that we have outgrown or that are unhealthy out of a misguided sense of loyalty. What are your thoughts on this? Besides misguided loyalty, what are some other reasons that people stay in relationships that are unhealthy or that they have long outgrown? What are some of the tell-tale signs that a relationship is no longer healthy or no longer contributing to your positive development? Is it possible to be loving and respectful to people who you no longer want in your inner circle? How can you maintain love and respect while still choosing to distance yourself from them? Do you think that many women stay in dead relationships because they're afraid to be alone?

19. In Motivational Morsel #40. *If Real Love Showed Up Would You Be Ready*, the author says that some of us are so addicted to dysfunction and drama that we are not able to appreciate a good thing until it's gone. Do you agree with this statement? Why or why not? What do you think that some people are more attracted to drama than others? What does real love look and feel like to you? Would you be ready? The author also talks about the law of attraction and how what you draw to you is what you are. Do you believe in the law of attraction? If yes, why? If not, then what pulls people together or attracts two people to each other? Do you believe in giving yourself a little downtime after a relationship? What are the benefits of taking a little downtime before entering into a new relationship? How much downtime should one take?

20. In Motivational Morsel #42. *Does He Love You Enough To Wipe Your Behind*, the author shares a story about her grandmother's advice on how to select a mate. What advice and lessons have you received concerning how to select a mate? What advice and lessons have you passed on to other women concerning how to select a mate? Where do we get our ideas about love and intimacy from? In your opinion, what are the key ingredients to a loving, lasting relationship? Do you think it's more difficult to find true love than it was during your parents and grandparents generation? What are some of the challenges to finding love in today's fast-paced, instant gratification culture? How can we address and, or work through these challenges in order to find the love that so many women are hoping to find?

Tips for Starting Your Own Women's Reading Group

- Go on line and do a google search for women's reading groups. See if any exist in your community. If so, find out if they are accepting new members and what you need to do to join. Then recommend this book for one of the discussions.

- Reach out to women who you feel connected to or have a good feeling about. Tell them about your desire to start a women's reading group designed to bring women together for social interaction, empowering dialogue and "me time." Ask for their thoughts and ideas.

- Decide on the group size, how often the group will meet, where the group will meet. Find out what the women want to get out of the reading group and let their feedback serve as your guide.

- Choose a group coordinator who is committed to seeing the group through, who will keep the group connected and who is willing to put in the work to get the group off the ground.

- Ask each group member to recommend a book. Once titles are selected, ask everyone to purchase or borrow the book from the library and read it by the next meeting date.

- Ask each group member to come up with two to three questions or issues relevant to the selected book that they would like to discuss at the next meeting. Then, use their questions as a springboard for your discussion. For this book, *The Busy Woman's Little Book of Motivation,* discussion questions are provided in the back of the book.

Suggestions for Your First Meeting

- As the women arrive you should receive them with a warm welcome. You can have music playing in the background and maybe a photo album that they can look through while they are waiting for the other women to arrive.

- When all of the women arrive, you can begin with a 10 to 15 minute icebreaker to help the women break the ice with one another.

- Begin the book discussion with each woman selecting a question from the book discussion guide section in this book. For other readings make up your own questions and have a dialogue around the relevant issues and themes.

- Schedule the next meeting. Distribute a group members list to all of the women with everyone's names, telephone numbers, emails and birthdays.

About The Author

Cassandra Mack is president and CEO of *Strategies for Empowered Living Inc.*, a New York based motivational speaking, training and consulting company that offers workshops, keynotes and products in 4 areas: the empowerment of girls and women, youth development, personal growth and supervisory skills.

Cassandra has conducted keynotes, break-out sessions and business seminars for regional, state and national conferences and conventions. Some of the organizations she has worked with include: Xerox, TIAA-Cref, The National Mentoring Partnership, The Support Center for Nonprofit Management, Child Welfare League of America, National Resource Center for Youth Services, Big Brothers Big Sisters, Covenant House, NYC Department of Education, Archdiocese Drug Abuse Prevention Program,

For more information about Cassandra Mack's workshops, books, audiotapes and internet radio show go to her website: **www.strategiesforempoweredliving.com**

Listen To Cassandra Mack Live
On Internet Radio!!!

You can listen to Cassandra Mack live on internet radio every Monday from 12noon to 1pm eastern standard time as she tackles real life issues on her popular call-in talk radio show **The No More Drama Hour of Power....**

From accelerating your career, building wealth and dealing with workplace drama to dating, mating, relating and cohabitating Cassandra Mack, brings the issues to you straight with no chaser. So don't miss one episode of **The No More Drama Hour of Power.** The drama you avoid may be your own.

To access Cassandra's show go to her website: **www.strategiesforempoweredliving.com** and click on the radio show link.

Other Books By The Author

The Single Mom's Little Book of Wisdom.
The Single Mom's Little Moms Little Book of Wisdom offers 42 insightful principles that will encourage any single mother to succeed, survive and stay strong.

The Single Mom's Little Book of Wisdom Companion Workbook.
This is the 8 ½ by 11companion workbook to *The Single Mom's Little Book of Wisdom* The companion workbook will show you how to move from principle to practice.

Cool, Confident and Strong: 52 Power Moves for Girls.
This book provides pre-teen and teenage girls with the tools they need to take decisions that respect their values and boundaries.

Young, Gifted and Doing It: 52 Power Moves for Teens.
From resisting peer pressure to setting goals and making education a top priority, this book is the definitive success guide for teens.

Smart Moves That Successful Youth Workers Make.
In this book you'll learn: the 7 roles of the front-line youth worker, how to avoid the 10 biggest mistakes smart youth workers make and how to build assets in youth.

Smart Moves That Successful Managers Make.
In this book you'll learn how to lead and manage more effectively. You'll learn how to identify the 12 common mistakes well-meaning managers make and put a system in place to increase productivity in yourself and your employees.

Audio Programs By The Author

10 Foolish Mistakes Smart Single Moms Make

From using the children as pawns to trying to be all things to all people, this audio CD gives you the real deal on how to let go of the attitudes and behaviors that can sabotage your success as a parent and as a person on the path to excellence.

What Smart Women Know: The 9 Essentials That Will Position You To Prosper

This audio CD offers 9 powerful principles that will position you to achieve lifelong success and abundant living.

978-0-595-49780-5
0-595-49780-2

Lightning Source UK Ltd.
Milton Keynes UK
28 December 2010

164958UK00001B/144/P